Blanche Willis Howard, Theobald Gross

The Humming Top

Debit And Credit in the Next World

Blanche Willis Howard, Theobald Gross

The Humming Top
Debit And Credit in the Next World

ISBN/EAN: 9783744725705

Printed in Europe, USA, Canada, Australia, Japan

Cover: Foto ©Suzi / pixelio.de

More available books at **www.hansebooks.com**

THE HUMMING TOP, OR DEBIT AND CREDIT IN THE NEXT WORLD

Translated by
BLANCHE WILLIS HOWARD
AUTHOR OF "ONE SUMMER," "GUENN," ETC.

NEW YORK
FREDERICK A. STOKES COMPANY
MDCCCXC

THE HUMMING TOP, OR DEBIT AND CREDIT IN THE NEXT WORLD

[Authorized Translation from the German of Theobald Gross.]

BY

BLANCHE

WILLIS

HOWARD

COUNT GEIERFLUG, the mightiest minister of the realm, had breathed his last. His final moments on earth had left him looking somewhat pale and worn, but had in no respect diminished his pride, or the aristocratic elegance of his bearing.

Attired in a gold-embroidered coat, such as men of his distinction are apt to wear when lying in funereal state, he started off on the direct road to Heaven.

Marching along at a brisk pace, he presently overtook and passed a little group consisting of three most wretched beings; a white-haired, palsied old pauper woman, a youth, from whose neck still dangled the halter which he had brought with him from the closing scene of his life drama, and a poor little hump-backed consumptive boy, five or six years old, who, from time to time glanced lovingly at a toy clasped close in his wasted hand.

Count Geierflug arrived at the gates of Heaven, and politely addressed Saint Peter:

" Pardon me," he began, " I would merely beg to inquire—"

But the former apostle and present keeper of the celestial gates interrupted him sternly:

" It's not your turn. The three behind

there, whom you passed on the road, come
first.''

"Before *me*? I am Count Geierflug, the prime-minister.   I have the title of Excellency, am knight of innumerable orders, member of various learned societies and—"

"Up here we recognize neither knight nor scholar."

"But your Reverence was a kind of knight yourself, and wielded a dashing blade in the affair with Malchus."

Peter silently regarded the smiling speaker.

"And your Reverence was also a *quasi* scholar—or author—or—"

"On earth I was only a poor fisherman."

"And yet," continued the Count, with a profound bow, "your Reverence's Epistles are even more celebrated than the world-renowned letters of Madame de Sévigné."

Again Peter surveyed the flatterer in utter silence, but with so penetrating a gaze that the false courtier-eyes drooped beneath it.

In the mean time, the three pilgrims had arrived.

No sooner did Saint Peter see the boy's innocent face and crippled body than he said kindly:

"Run in, little one. This is the right place for you."

The Apostle then turned to a thick book,

upon which, in golden letters, stood
" Ledger."

" What is your name ?" he asked the old
woman.

" Brigitte Stegmaierin, if you please, holy
Saint Peter," she replied, with a courtesy.

" Precisely — Brigitte Stegmaierin," re-
peated Saint Peter, poring over his Ledger.
Then, in a grumbling tone, he continued :

"Debit: 'Has a bitter, bad tongue of her own.' While—h'm! charged to her Credit —is:—'She is grievously poor.'"

"Poor!" cried the old crone, weeping and flinging up her arms; "God is my witness that is true; and holy Saint Peter himself knows poverty is a gnawing pain. Poverty sweetens nobody's temper."

"Well, well," said the Apostle gently; "go in, granny—go in. In there, there is no more poverty or pain."

The young man with the halter around his neck now stepped forward.

"Your name," demanded Saint Peter.

"Veit Krätzern."

"Stole a gold bracelet," read the Apostle with a frown.

"*Item:* A purse full of money.

"*Item:* The contents of the contribution box at St. James' church."

St. Peter scowled fiercely at the youth who shook like a leaf in the blast.

"Credited : 'He did it all at the instigation and entreaty of his sweetheart.' H'm ! Did you love the woman so very much ?"

"Ah!" faltered the boy, "I could never tell you how much! I—"

"Enough!" broke in Saint Peter. "Don't talk to me about it. Be off, will you? Out of my sight!"

"What! In there?" and the thief pointed toward the gates.

"Well—yes. Only make haste or I may repent my weakness."

Through the briefly opened portals the fair forms and pitiful faces of two shining angels were revealed. One of them tenderly wiped the tears from poor old Brigitte's eyes, while the other, murmuring mild and compassionate words removed the rope from Veit Krätzern's neck.

"Now we are ready for you," remarked Saint Peter to the Count, turning over leaf after leaf of the Ledger, and suddenly exclaiming in a horrified tone :

"That looks promising, indeed! Column after column of Debit items, while nothing stands to your Credit—absolutely nothing!"

The Count began pompously:

"I have advanced the commerce, manufactures and agriculture of my native land. I have protected and promoted the arts and sciences. I have built churches and schools and orphan asylums and hospitals and poorhouses and—"

"Peace, fool!" cried Saint Peter angrily. "All that is charged fast enough, not to your credit but against you, because it was done from ambition and selfishness and ostentation and hypocrisy."

"My life's best work," continued the Count, still more proudly, "how I made my fatherland great and glorious beyond all lands on earth I do not need to mention, for I presume my fame has long ago ascended here."

"Your fame," retorted Saint Peter with increasing indignation, "has not reached us, but the groans of dying youths have risen to us from your battle-fields and from desolate homes, the despair of mothers and brides; and I tell you, wretch, if you have nothing better than this to urge, you are a lost man!"

The Count grew still paler, and had not a word to say for himself.

At this moment the little boy, lingering on the threshold of Heaven, called out:

" Mr. Peter ! Mr. Peter ! "

" Are you still there, my little man ? " returned the Apostle; " why do you not enter ? "

Instead of replying to the question, the little fellow said :

" Mr. Peter, do you see this humming-top ? "

Pulling the string he sent the top flying from the handle and spinning about with a jolly hum at the feet of the Apostle and the Count.

" Upon my word!   A real humming-top," Saint Peter returned indulgently. " Pray how came it here ? "

" My mother laid it in my grave with me," answered the child seriously.   He then picked up his top, re-wound the string, and extending the toy temptingly toward the Apostle, said :

" Mr. Peter, if you will let the Count go in there with me, I will let you spin my top."

" Do you know the Count, child ? "

" Of course. It was the Count that gave me my top."

" Ah! Tell me how that happened, dear boy."

" Once I was sitting at the door eating my bread. And when I had finished I began to cry. Just then the Count came driving along in a beautiful blue and gold coach with four gray horses. And the carriage stopped, and the Count said:

"'Are you hungry, little boy?'

"'No,' said I, 'I have just had my bread.'

"And the Count said, 'Then why are you crying?'

"And then I said, 'I am so lonely. Father and mother go off to work early in the morning and don't come home till late at night, and the children won't play with me because I am so slow.' Then the Count said that he would bring me something to play with. And in a little while he came back with the top, and we made it spin, the Count and I together; and after that I never cried any more."

Saint Peter made no reply, but buried his head in his Ledger, muttering:

"I know he's rather old fogyish in his accounts, our old book-keeper, Gabriel—still, we have always been able to rely upon him—ah, I was sure of it!" he exclaimed joyfully : " here it is on the very last Credit page :

" ' Gave a day-laborer's crippled child a toy—commonly called a humming-top—and with great kindness and gentleness showed the boy how to spin it." '

With almost youthful eagerness Saint Peter seized his red pencil, and drew a broad line through the whole long list of sins and transgressions, and the next moment the Count, clasping the child's hand, entered the Kingdom of Heaven.